A New Zimbabwe?

Assessing Continuity and Change
After Mugabe

ALEXANDER H. NOYES

Prepared for the James Harmon Foundation

RAND NATIONAL SECURITY RESEARCH DIVISION

For more information on this publication, visit www.rand.org/t/RR4367

Library of Congress Cataloging-in-Publication Data is available for this publication.
ISBN: 978-1-9774-0434-3

Published by the RAND Corporation, Santa Monica, Calif.
© Copyright 2020 RAND Corporation
RAND® is a registered trademark.

Cover:
Flag: enigma images/Getty Images/iStockphoto;
Mugabe: Kopano Tlape/flickr.

Support RAND
Make a tax-deductible charitable contribution at
www.rand.org/giving/contribute

www.rand.org

Preface

President Emmerson Mnangagwa of Zimbabwe came to office on the back of a military coup in November 2017, replacing President Robert Mugabe, who was in power for 37 years. Mnangagwa promised to take the country—mired in political and economic crisis for nearly two decades—in a new direction. Has he delivered? This report takes stock of Zimbabwe's political and economic reform efforts since Mugabe's departure and offers recommendations for how to help the country recover.

This research was sponsored by the James Harmon Foundation and conducted within the International Security and Defense Policy Center of the RAND National Security Research Division (NSRD). NSRD conducts research and analysis for the Office of the Secretary of Defense, the Joint Staff, the Unified Combatant Commands, the defense agencies, the Navy, the Marine Corps, the U.S. Coast Guard, the U.S. Intelligence Community, allied foreign governments, and foundations.

For more information on the RAND International Security and Defense Policy Center, see www.rand.org/nsrd/ndri/centers/isdp or contact the director (contact information is provided on the webpage).

Contents

Summary

After 37 years in power, President Robert Mugabe of Zimbabwe was toppled via a military coup in November 2017. His successor and former vice president, Emmerson Mnangagwa, promised a break from Mugabe's authoritarian rule and economic mismanagement, declaring a "new Zimbabwe" that is "open for business."[1] After two years in power, to what extent has Mnangagwa delivered on his promises? Where is the country headed? Is Zimbabwe on the road to becoming a fully fledged democracy or will it remain semiauthoritarian? Will its economy stabilize or deteriorate further? What are the opportunities and challenges for international reengagement and investment?

This report analyzes Zimbabwe's political and economic reform efforts after Mugabe. It also provides a forecast of the country's likely trajectory in the lead up to elections in 2023 and recommendations for the international community to help Zimbabwe recover from decades of autocratic misrule and international ostracization. While drawing on a variety of primary and secondary sources, the study uses elite interviews as the principal method of data collection.[2] The author conducted more than two dozen semistructured interviews in Harare, Zimbabwe, and Washington, D.C., in July and August 2019. Interviewees included current and former senior government and opposition

---

[1] Richard Quest and Sheena McKenzie, "President Mnangagwa: Zimbabwe is Open for Business," CNN, January 24, 2018.

[2] *Elite interviews* target people directly involved in the political process. They are used as a tool to tap into political processes that would otherwise be difficult to examine (Glenn Beamer, "Elite Interviews and State Politics Research," *State Politics and Policy Quarterly*, Vol. 2, No. 1, Spring 2002).

officials, nongovernmental experts, senior members of the diplomatic community, and industry leaders.

"Mascara on a Frog": Continuity Over Change

Due to a highly cartelized and patronage-based economy, politics and economics are inseparable in Zimbabwe. Although the Mnangagwa government has taken some modest steps that could be seen as an indication of progress—particularly on the economic front—there is a wide gap between the government's reform rhetoric and the reality on the ground. The government's pledges have fallen short, as genuine reform has been extremely sluggish and repression has increased under Mnangagwa. These well-rehearsed slogans appear to be largely political theater targeted at the international diplomatic community and investors.

Even where modest progress has been made, such steps appear to be largely cosmetic in many cases, a box-ticking exercise directed mainly at international actors rather than any real commitment to reform. In other words, Mnangagwa is attempting to have his cake and eat it, too, paying lip service to reforms in the hope of securing international support but staunchly refusing to implement any measures that might harm his and his closest supporters' political and economic interests. A serving member of parliament characterized Mnangagwa's reform efforts as putting "mascara on a frog."[3]

Little Movement on Political Reform

On the political front, reform promises are severely lagging, with very few tangible steps toward reconfiguring Zimbabwe's autocratic system. In August 2019, a senior diplomat said that none of the ten major legislative reforms that the government had promised had been fully implemented.[4] The government has taken steps to repeal and replace two repressive pieces of legislation, the Public Order and Security Act and the Access to Information and Protection of Privacy Act. However, the

---

[3]   Author interview, Harare, Zimbabwe, July 31, 2019.

[4]   Author interview with senior diplomat, Harare, Zimbabwe, August 1, 2019.

Mnangagwa government continues to prevent and violently suppress political protests and the media remain heavily biased in favor of the ruling party, as do the justice and electoral system.

A brief opening of political space in the run-up to the 2018 elections rapidly shut in the postelection period, when six protestors were killed by security forces and tanks deployed on Harare's streets for the second time in nine months. Several interviewees said that Mnangagwa is in many ways governing in a more repressive manner than Mugabe.[5] Security forces have cracked down on several occasions since Mnangagwa came to power, with more than 20 people killed and more than 1,000 arrested. Despite calls to hold perpetrators to account, the government has not prosecuted security forces and has stymied any real discussion of security sector reform.

Indeed, the military is on the ascendancy. Although the military has always played a prominent role in Zimbabwe's political economy, its influence has increased under Mnangagwa. The military remains heavily involved in the economy, particularly in the mining and fuel sectors. Two of the main figures behind the 2017 coup, former generals Constantino Chiwenga and Sibusiso Busi Moyo, are vice president and foreign minister, respectively, and remain powerful players representing military interests in Zimbabwe's cabinet.

Halting Movement on Piecemeal Economic Reform Amid Collapse

On the economic front, Mnangagwa's administration has taken steps toward a few piecemeal reforms in several areas, but progress has lagged in others. The fundamentals of the economy remain poor and the results of these patchwork reforms have not been promising thus far. Despite a brief government surplus and the introduction of a new currency aimed at curbing inflation, the economy is again close to collapse, with fuel, food, and electricity shortages reminiscent of Zimbabwe's political and economic crisis in the mid- to late 2000s. Several reform efforts remain unresolved, partial, or incomplete, including the highly contentious issues of land reform, corruption, mining, and

---

[5]   Author interviews, Harare, Zimbabwe, July 25–August 3, 2019.

privatization. Political manipulation and distortion of the economy continue.

In February 2019, in a step toward reestablishing a national currency, the government introduced the RTGS (Real-Time Gross Settlement) dollar and unpegged it from the U.S. dollar. The RTGS began trading at 1:3 against the U.S. dollar, but it rapidly devalued thereafter and reached levels of 1:16 in August 2019. In June 2019, the government banned all use of other currencies except for the RTGS. The move to the RTGS currency and its subsequent devaluation cut salaries and purchasing power by at least tenfold, meaning that, twice in the past two decades, Zimbabweans' savings accounts have largely been wiped out. In July 2019, the government abruptly stopped publishing official statistics. In August 2019, the International Monetary Fund estimated the inflation rate at 300 percent.[6] Some scholars put this figure much higher.

Many interviewees emphasized Zimbabweans' acute distrust of the government, particularly in regard to the management of the economy. After decades of monetary and fiscal mismanagement, record levels of inflation, rampant corruption, and slashed savings accounts, Zimbabweans have approached the recent switch back to a national currency with extreme trepidation. Wildly fluctuating exchange rates and a robust parallel market have also led to widespread currency arbitrage, with those who have access to foreign exchange—often government officials—reaping large profits.[7] A further indication that reform efforts are not meaningful is the choice of the country's large diaspora to remain abroad and not invest significant money back into the country.

---

6   International Monetary Fund, "IMF Staff Concludes Visit for the Article IV Consultation and Discussions on the First Review of the Staff-Monitored Program to Zimbabwe," press release No. 19/355, Washington, D.C., September 26, 2019.

7   Author interviews, Harare, Zimbabwe, July 25–August 3, 2019.

Forecast and Recommendations

Politics and economics are inextricably linked in Zimbabwe. With the old guard and the military still firmly in power—both benefiting from their perches atop the highly cartelized and patronage-based economy—genuine reform is unlikely in the next one to three years in the lead-up to national elections in 2023. Zimbabwe is likely to continue down a path of political polarization, protests, political violence at the hands of the state, and economic deterioration.

Recommendations

Zimbabwe has tremendous potential, with rich natural resources and one of the most educated populations in Africa. To help the country recover from decades of mismanagement, corruption, and state violence, international actors—including the United States—would be wise to push the government in a coordinated fashion to implement genuine political, economic, and security reforms. Such reforms would go a long way toward putting Zimbabwe on a democratic path, lowering levels of political polarization, and repairing the collapsing economy. Reforms would also reassure potential investors and help to earn back the goodwill—and possible access to lending—of the international community.

Acknowledgments

I would like to offer a big thank you to James Harmon and the James Harmon Foundation for sponsoring this report and providing helpful feedback throughout the research process. Thanks also to Cornelius Queen for helping to usher the project through its various phases. I would also like to offer great thanks and appreciation to the many interlocutors and stakeholders who took the time to talk in Zimbabwe and Washington, D.C.; this project would not have been possible without their generosity and candor. I would also like to thank Stephanie Pezard of RAND and an anonymous external reviewer for providing insightful comments and suggestions.

Abbreviations

DRC	Democratic Republic of the Congo
G40	Generation 40
GDP	gross domestic product
MDC	Movement for Democratic Change
RTGS	Real-Time Gross Settlement
POSA	Public Order and Security Act
ZACC	Zimbabwe Anti-Corruption Commission
ZANU-PF	Zimbabwe African National Union-Patriotic Front
ZEC	Zimbabwe Election Commission

CHAPTER ONE

Introduction

After 37 years in power, President Robert Mugabe of Zimbabwe was toppled via a military coup in November 2017. His successor and former vice president, Emmerson Mnangagwa, promised a break from Mugabe's authoritarian rule and economic mismanagement, declaring a "new Zimbabwe" that is "open for business."[1] After two years in power, to what extent has Mnangagwa delivered on his promises? Where is the country headed? Is Zimbabwe on the road to becoming a fully fledged democracy or will it remain semiauthoritarian? Will its economy stabilize or deteriorate further? What are the opportunities and challenges for international reengagement and investment?

Scope and Methodology

This report provides an analysis of the Mnangagwa administration's political and economic reform efforts over the past two years since Mugabe's ouster. In the concluding section, the report offers a forecast of the country's likely trajectory over the next one to three years in the lead-up to presidential and parliamentary elections scheduled for 2023. It also offers recommendations for the international community to help Zimbabwe recover from decades of autocratic misrule and

---

[1] Richard Quest and Sheena McKenzie, "President Mnangagwa: Zimbabwe Is Open for Business," CNN, January 24, 2018.

international ostracization. Elite interviews[2] were used as the principal method of data collection for this study, in addition to drawing on a variety of primary and secondary sources. The author conducted more than two dozen semistructured interviews in Harare, Zimbabwe, and Washington, D.C., in July and August 2019. Interviewees included current and former senior government and opposition officials, nongovernmental experts, senior members of the diplomatic community, and industry leaders. The research followed RAND's Human Subjects Protection Committee guidelines. Consent was secured prior to each interview, data protection safeguards were used throughout, and interviewees have been anonymized in the report to protect sources.

Brief History

Zimbabwe is a landlocked, lower-middle income country located in southern Africa with a population of 14 million.[3] In 2018, it had a gross domestic product (GDP) of $25.8 billion. This 2018 figure was revised upward significantly when the government rebased the economy in an effort to capture output from the large informal sector, boosting GDP to its current level from $18 billion in 2017.[4] Zimbabwe is a semiauthoritarian country, with power concentrated in the executive. The country regularly holds flawed elections, with the playing field skewed in favor of the incumbent Zimbabwe African National Union–Patriotic Front (ZANU-PF) party. A bloody liberation war fought against Rhodesia was ended by the Lancaster House Agreement in 1979 and followed by Zimbabwe's independence in 1980. Mugabe won the country's founding elections and stayed in power until he was

---

[2]   *Elite interviews* target people directly involved in the political process. They are used as a tool to tap into political processes that would otherwise be difficult to examine (Glenn Beamer, "Elite Interviews and State Politics Research," *State Politics and Policy Quarterly*, Vol. 2, No. 1, Spring 2002).

[3]   World Bank, "Zimbabwe," webpage, undated.

[4]   MacDonald Dzirutwe, "Zimbabwe Rebases Data, Boosting GDP Numbers by 40 pct," *Reuters*, October 5, 2018.

overthrown in November 2017. Mugabe died in September 2019 after being treated for cancer in Singapore.

Zimbabwe has a strong party-military alliance—bound together by a shared liberation ideology, extensive corruption, and patronage networks—and a long history of political violence at the hands of the state.[5] More than 20,000 were killed by security forces in the early 1980s in a campaign of violence known as the *Gukurahundi*.[6] Despite this mass violence, Mugabe's first decade and a half in office was held up by international actors as a postconflict success story and a shining example of racial reconciliation.[7] The economy expanded, and Zimbabwe was often referred to as the "breadbasket" of the region. This honeymoon period came to an end in the late 1990s. Led by the late Morgan Tsvangirai, the opposition Movement for Democratic Change (MDC) party was founded in 1999 in response to rising discontent with corruption, rapid economic decline, and an unpopular military deployment to the Democratic Republic of the Congo (DRC).

In 2000, the MDC won a surprise victory against ZANU-PF when it defeated a constitutional referendum aimed at granting further powers to Mugabe. Faced with his first real political threat since independence, Mugabe and his party-military alliance reacted with an iron fist. They cracked down on dissent, orchestrated a series of violent elections, violently expropriated land from white farmers without compensation, engaged in large-scale corruption, and printed money to pay off veterans of the liberation war and distribute patronage to other key bases of support. These actions precipitated a political and economic crisis and earned Zimbabwe pariah status on the international stage, with the United States and the European Union levying targeted sanctions on dozens of officials—including Mugabe and

---

[5]   Human Rights Watch, *Perpetual Fear: Impunity and Cycles of Violence in Zimbabwe*, New York, March 8, 2011.

[6]   Catholic Commission for Justice and Peace, *Breaking the Silence, Building True Peace: A Report on the Disturbances in Matabeleland and the Midlands, 1980 to 1988 Summary Report*, Harare, Zimbabwe: Legal Resources Foundation, 1999.

[7]   Blessing-Miles Tendi, "Robert Mugabe and Toxicity: History and Context Matter," *Representation*, Vol. 47, No. 3, 2011.

Mnangagwa—responsible for human rights abuses. The crisis came to a head in 2008, when the country set records for hyperinflation and the economy neared total collapse.[8]

Tsvangirai of the MDC won a first-round victory in the 2008 elections. But after a month delay, the electoral commission announced that a second round was necessary because neither candidate allegedly reached the required 50 percent of the votes. Mugabe and ZANU-PF, with a leading role played by Mnangagwa, then unleashed a campaign of violence that left more than 200 dead and thousands injured.[9] Tsvangirai withdrew amid the violence, handing Mugabe a victory that was seen as illegitimate, leading to a power-sharing accord between Mugabe and Tsvangirai—brokered by the Southern African Development Community. The power-sharing government, which kept Mugabe as president and installed Tsvangirai in the newly created post of prime minister, was in office from 2009 to 2013.

Under power-sharing, Zimbabwe dollarized and the economy stabilized, with double-digit growth overseen by MDC Finance Minister Tendai Biti. Zimbabwe also briefly enjoyed a period of rapprochement with the international community. Yet, with the exception of a new constitution in 2013, Mugabe and ZANU-PF fiercely resisted reform efforts during the power-sharing period, winning elections in 2013 that the opposition claimed were rigged.[10] Firmly back in sole control of the country, ZANU-PF in the ensuing years became consumed by a leadership succession struggle that would eventually lead to Mugabe's overthrow.

In 2014, Mugabe sacked his vice president, Joice Mujuru, and replaced her with longtime confidant Mnangagwa, who has a long history as one of Mugabe's staunchest supporters. Mnangagwa served

---

8   Tendai Biti, "History Repeats Itself in Zimbabwe," *Foreign Affairs*, August 20, 2019.

9   Human Rights Watch, *Perpetual Fear: Impunity and Cycles of Violence in Zimbabwe*, New York, March 8, 2011.

10   Alexander Noyes, "*Plus ça Change?* The Dynamics of Security Sector Reform in Zimbabwe, 2009–2013," in Blessing-Miles Tendi, Jocelyn Alexander, and JoAnn McGregor, eds., *The Oxford Handbook of Zimbabwean Studies*, Oxford, UK: Oxford University Press: forthcoming.

as Mugabe's aide prior to independence and held various senior government roles thereafter, including as minister of state for national security during the *Gukurahundi* massacre in the 1980s and later as minister of defense and minister of justice. Mnangagwa is a crucial player in Zimbabwe's enduring party-military alliance that has kept ZANU-PF in power for nearly four decades. He is also considered to be one of the wealthiest people in the country, with extensive commercial interests—including in diamonds, gold mining, and fuel—and connections to controversial local and foreign business figures.[11] He was named by a United Nations panel as a key player in Zimbabwe's deployment to the DRC conflict in 1998, where Zimbabwean military and political officials were accused of plundering natural resources, earning them the title of "conflict entrepreneurs."[12] A former politician described Mnangagwa as "Mugabe's brains all these years, a master of duplicity and intrigue."[13]

Shortly after becoming vice president, a rivalry developed between Mnangagwa and Mugabe's wife, Grace Mugabe. The faction aligned with Mnangagwa, which had backing from senior members of the military (including Zimbabwe Defence Forces commander Constantino Chiwenga), came to be known as Lacoste. The faction headed by Grace Mugabe, which featured several younger officials without liberation war credentials, took on the moniker Generation 40 (G40). Meanwhile, after double-digit growth during the power-sharing period, the economy again began to deteriorate after Mugabe and ZANU-PF regained complete control and installed party stalwart Patrick Chinamasa as minister of finance.

Amid increasingly open hostility between Lacoste and G40, Mugabe's alliance with the military and liberation war veterans began to fray. In 2016, the Zimbabwe National Liberation War Veterans

---

[11] Blair Rutherford, "Mugabe's Shadow: Limning the Penumbrae of Post-Coup Zimbabwe, *Canadian Journal of African Studies*, Vol. 52, No. 1, 2018.

[12] Paul Jackson, "The Civil War Roots of Military Domination in Zimbabwe: The Integration Process Following the Rhodesian War and the Road to ZANLA Dominance," *Civil Wars*, Vol. 13, No. 4, 2011.

[13] Author interview, Harare, Zimbabwe, July 26, 2019.

Association publicly broke with Mugabe, condemning his dictatorial ways and alleging that he had abandoned the values of the liberation struggle. Powerful actors within the military also began to drift from Mugabe, with some politically ambitious generals considering a coup to reestablish the preeminence of the liberation war ethos in the party and protect their interests.[14] Mugabe's tight grip on the longstanding—and heretofore mutually beneficial—party-military alliance was slipping.

These growing tensions came to a head with Mugabe's firing of Mnangagwa on November 6, 2017, which was viewed as a step toward Grace Mugabe and the G40 moving into the driver's seat of the succession struggle. Mugabe's refusal to dialogue with the military on November 13, 2017, to resolve their differences was the final catalyst for the coup, with Chiwenga and others launching Operation Restore Legacy the following day, leading to Mugabe's resignation on November 21, 2017.[15] After 37 years in power, Mugabe, the master tactician, had finally overplayed his hand. Mnangagwa, who fled to Mozambique and South Africa after his firing, was sworn in on November 24, 2017.

---

[14]   Blessing-Miles Tendi, "The Motivations and Dynamics of Zimbabwe's 2017 Military Coup," *African Affairs*, Vol. 24, October 28, 2019.

[15]   Tendi, 2019.

CHAPTER TWO

Politics After Mugabe

Overview

After taking office, despite Mnangagwa playing a leading role in Mugabe's government for 37 years since independence, he promised a sharp departure from his erstwhile ally's brutal and authoritarian style of rule. Early on in his administration, Mnangagwa pledged to implement a raft of political and economic reforms and began a public relations charm offensive aimed at reengagement with the international community. He often repeated slogans highlighting that Zimbabwe was under a "new dispensation," whereby he would allow political competition, cease repression, deliver free and fair elections, and invite international monitors back into the fold.[1] His campaign for the July 2018 elections doubled down on these proclamations. After two years in office, has Mnangagwa lived up to these promises?

"Mascara on a Frog": Little Movement on Political Reform

Despite some confrontational rhetoric—particularly around the issue of international sanctions—the Mnangagwa government and top ZANU-PF leadership do want improved relations with the United States and other Western countries. In interviews, government and

---

[1] Quest and McKenzie, 2018.

party officials unwaveringly toed the party line, reiterating Mnangagwa's reform agenda and openly calling for international reengagement and the lifting of sanctions.[2] But an analysis of Mnangagwa's record demonstrates that these reform promises are severely lagging, with very few tangible steps toward reconfiguring Zimbabwe's autocratic system and breaking from Mugabe's corrupt and patronage-based rule. In an apt description, a serving member of parliament characterized Mnangagwa's reform efforts as putting "mascara on a frog."[3]

Elections

In the run-up to the 2018 elections, there was a brief opening of political space when Nelson Chamisa of the MDC and other candidates were able to campaign freely, even in ZANU-PF strongholds that previously would have been off limits to the opposition. A current minister described the 2018 campaign as a period of "unprecedented freedoms."[4] Mnangagwa followed through on his promise to invite international election observers from Western countries—a first since the early 2000s—and overhauled the outdated voter rolls, which were heavily criticized in the 2013 elections. However, old ZANU-PF habits proved to die hard, because the 2018 campaign was also marked by a series of significant flaws. The electoral playing field remained acutely uneven, with local and international observers highlighting that the Zimbabwe Electoral Commission (ZEC) lacked independence, the media remained partisan toward ZANU-PF, the new voter rolls showed signs of manipulation, and security forces intimidated citizens.[5] With memories of the November 2017 coup fresh for Zimbabweans, the role of the military continued to loom large in the country. In a poll held prior to the 2018 election, 44 percent of Zimbabweans said it was "some-

---

2 Author interviews, Harare, Zimbabwe, July 25–August 3, 2019.

3 Author interview, Harare, Zimbabwe, July 31, 2019.

4 Author interview, Harare, Zimbabwe, July 30, 2019.

5 International Republican Institute and National Democratic Institute, *IRI/NDI Zimbabwe International Election Observation Mission: Final Report*, Washington, D.C., October 2018.

what" or "very" likely that security agencies would not respect the will of the people.[6]

Although election day itself was peaceful, with a high turnout of more than 70 percent, this brief window of political opening rapidly shut in the postelection period, when security forces killed six and injured a dozen (see the "Repression" section later in this chapter). On August 2, 2018, the ZEC declared Mnangagwa as the winner with 50.8 percent of the vote (this figure was later revised down to 50.67 percent) to Chamisa's 44.3 percent, meaning Mnangagwa narrowly avoided a second round. Overall, although noting some improvements in the 2018 election, the U.S. election observation mission (on which the author served as a delegate) expressed "deep concerns that the process has not made the mark."[7]

Legislation

Repressive legislation has long been used by ZANU-PF as a tool to suppress opposition and maintain an unlevel playing field. Repressive legislation remained on the books in the election period, with the long-standing Public Order and Security Act (POSA) being invoked prior to the military's deployment on August 1, 2018. Since the election, the government has taken steps to repeal and replace POSA and the Access to Information and Protection of Privacy Act, two pieces of legislation that have faced internal and external criticism for being undemocratic and repressive. Yet the Mnangagwa government continues to prevent and violently suppress political protests, and the media remain heavily biased in favor of the ruling party. Moreover, the replacements of these two bills have been sharply criticized by the opposition and civil society organizations as inadequate or unconstitutional. In August 2019, a senior diplomat said that none of the ten major legislative reforms that the government had promised had been fully implemented.[8] These

---

[6]   Afrobarometer and Mass Public Opinion Institute, "Zimbabweans Remain Apprehensive About Manipulation of the Presidential Election, New Survey Finds," press release, Harare, Zimbabwe, July 23, 2018.

[7]   International Republican Institute and National Democratic Institute, 2018, p. 53.

[8]   Author interview with senior diplomat, Harare, Zimbabwe, August 1, 2019.

bills touch on consumer protection, education, security, media, international treaties, and the constitutional court.

Repression

Human rights abuses, arrests, and disappearances of opposition members and supporters continue under Mnangagwa, with an uptick in state violence. Mnangagwa has deployed security forces to crack down on protests and dissent on several occasions since he came to power. On August 1, when the ZEC released parliamentary results showing ZANU-PF winning a two-thirds majority, opposition supporters demonstrated in downtown Harare, marching, burning tires, and throwing rocks at police. The military was deployed, with tanks rolling on Harare's streets for the second time in nine months. In a violent crackdown, the military killed six and injured more than a dozen. In the following weeks, security forces targeted opposition figures and supporters—with a series of kidnappings and disappearances—leading MDC Secretary General Tendai Biti to flee to Zambia. Despite calls by a government commission to hold perpetrators to account, security forces have not been prosecuted.

In January 2019, demonstrations in Harare over a surge in fuel prices were again met by excessive use of force. Seventeen people were killed, more than 1,000 were arrested, and 17 women were raped by security forces.[9] Several interviewees said that Mnangagwa is, in many ways, governing in a more repressive manner than Mugabe.[10] A senior diplomat described the "brazen nature" of security forces' behavior as "shocking," noting that joint military and intelligence teams now carry out kidnappings in broad daylight.[11]

Security Sector

Although the military has always played a prominent role in Zimbabwe's political economy, its influence has increased under Mnangagwa.

---

[9]   Human Rights Watch, "Zimbabwe: Excessive Force Used Against Protesters," webpage, March 12, 2019.

[10]   Author interviews, Harare, Zimbabwe, July 25–August 3, 2019.

[11]   Author interview, Harare, Zimbabwe, August 1, 2019.

The military remains heavily involved in the economy, particularly in the mining and fuel sectors.[12] Two of the main leaders of the 2017 coup, former generals Constantino Chiwenga and Sibusiso Busi Moyo, serve as vice president and foreign minister, respectively, and remain powerful players representing military interests in Zimbabwe's cabinet. Divides in Zimbabwe's security sector are not new. But the Mnangagwa administration has deliberately elevated the role of the military, with the police and intelligence service—which Mugabe frequently used for regime maintenance—losing influence and status in the security sector hierarchy.[13] Although the government has touted police trainings with the United Nations,[14] domestic and international calls for genuine security sector reform have been ignored or stymied. Indeed, the party-military alliance is alive and well in a post-Mugabe Zimbabwe. An opposition official noted that there is no separation between Mnangagwa and the military. The official said that Mnangagwa "uses the military to achieve his ends, commercially and politically."[15]

Judiciary

Zimbabwe's judiciary also has a long history of bias toward the ruling party. During the 2018 election period, lower courts issued several surprising rulings that indicated a degree of independence, yet many of those decisions were later overturned by higher courts.[16] The country's Constitutional Court ruled in November 2017 that the military coup was legal and decided in favor of Mnangagwa in August 2018 when the MDC contested the election results. The court has also handed down a number of other decisions in favor of the government and ruling party. After the elections, the Constitutional Court did rule that parts

---

[12] Nicole Beardsworth, Nic Cheeseman, and Simukai Tinhu, "Zimbabwe: The Coup That Never Was, and the Election That Could Have Been," *African Affairs*, Vol. 118, No. 472, September 2019, pp. 580–596.

[13] Author interviews, Harare, Zimbabwe, July 25–August 3, 2019.

[14] Author interview, Harare, Zimbabwe, July 31, 2019.

[15] Author interview, Harare, Zimbabwe, July 31, 2019.

[16] International Republican Institute and National Democratic Institute, 2018, p. 53.

of POSA were unconstitutional, yet the courts continue to rule in favor of banning opposition protests.

Judicial reforms have been slow, with the Constitutional Court bill, which will regulate the jurisdiction and powers of Zimbabwe's highest court, tabled in parliament but not yet passed. Moreover, according to a senior opposition official, the "Constitutional Court bill consolidates the power of the President. . . . It amends the Constitution instead of aligning laws with it."[17] A constitutional amendment, the Constitutional Amendment No. 2 Bill, tabled in parliament in December 2019, has also faced criticism from legal experts for aiming to strengthen the executive's control over judicial appointments.[18] Overall, despite a few glimmers of independence, Zimbabwe's judiciary remains firmly within ZANU-PF's sphere of influence. According to Freedom House: "In 2018, court decisions and other developments continued to suggest the strong influence of the executive and the ZANU-PF over the judiciary."[19] Indeed, a senior opposition official remarked that there has been "zero effort on judicial reform. The judiciary remains captured."[20]

Conclusion

In sum, despite a few cosmetic changes, the Mnangagwa administration has largely failed to overhaul Zimbabwe's political system. Promises for political reform have fallen short, with little movement in the areas of elections, legislation, human rights, and the partisan nature of state institutions, especially the security sector and judiciary. A senior diplomat in Harare said that there is a "global consensus that the government is not doing enough" on political reforms.[21] An opposition

---

[17] Author correspondence, November 3, 2019.

[18] Justice Alfred Mavedzenge, "Is Zimbabwe's President Mnangagwa Using Constitutional Amendments to Rig the 2023 Elections?" *Democracy in Africa*, January 22, 2020.

[19] Freedom House, "Zimbabwe," Washington, D.C., *Freedom in the World 2019*, February 2019.

[20] Author correspondence, November 3, 2019.

[21] Author interview, Harare, Zimbabwe, August 1, 2019.

figure echoed this sentiment, stating that political reforms that the Mnangagwa government has been touting are "piecemeal and fictional," a mere "ruse to sell to the international community."[22]

---

[22] Author interview, Harare, Zimbabwe, July 31, 2019.

CHAPTER THREE

Economics After Mugabe

Overview

Akin to the political front, Mnangagwa upon taking office promised several swift economic reforms aimed at reviving Zimbabwe's battered economy. Mnangagwa vowed to crack down on corruption, expand the economy through trade and investment, deal with massive external debt, and offer compensation on land reform.[1] Indeed, boosting the economy took center stage for Mnangagwa. In December 2017, he said: "From now on Zimbabwe is open for business. Yes, there will be political issues, but primarily it is economics, economics, economics, and trade for Zimbabwe."[2] His 2018 election campaign led with the "open for business" slogan. Have Mnangagwa and his administration delivered?

Halting Movement on Piecemeal Economic Reform Amid Collapse

Mnangagwa's administration has moved on various piecemeal reforms in a few economic sectors, but progress has lagged or been nonexistent

---

[1]   Quest and McKenzie, 2018.

[2]   "Zimbabwe Is Open for Business: Mnangagwa," SABC News, December 21, 2017.

in others. An analysis of Mnangagwa's economic record thus far shows that the fundamentals of the economy remain poor and the results of these few patchwork reforms have not been promising. Despite a very brief government surplus and the introduction of a new currency aimed at easing a liquidity crunch and curbing inflation, the economy is again close to collapse, with fuel, bread, and electricity shortages reminiscent of Zimbabwe's political and economic crisis in the late 2000s. Zimbabwe's GDP growth dropped from 3.5 percent in 2018 to −7 percent in 2019.[3]

Zimbabwe's large external debt burden of more than $9 billion, a poor climate for investment, and exceedingly high government wage expenses also hurt economic performance, as does policy inconsistency and a lack of reliable information from the government on financial, regulatory, and monetary policies. Severe drought and devastation wrought by cyclone Idai in March 2019 have further constrained the economy, with more than 2 million people facing starvation.[4] In sum, Mnangagwa's fragmented economic reform efforts have not been sufficient to arrest the sinking economy and instill confidence. A further indication that reform efforts are not meaningful is the lack of a returning diaspora. The country's large diaspora has chosen to remain abroad and has not significantly ramped up investment in the country. Although some interviewees were optimistic that government efforts would eventually change the direction of the economy, many others were much less sanguine. A Zimbabwean business leader remarked that the economic "reform agenda is cosmetic at best."[5]

Currency and Inflation

In February 2019, in a step toward reestablishing a national currency, the government introduced the RTGS (Real-Time Gross Settlement) dollar and unpegged it from the U.S. dollar in a partial float. The RTGS began trading at 1:3 against the U.S. dollar, but it rapidly deval-

---

[3]   World Bank, undated.

[4]   Mark Chingono and Bukola Adebayo, "Millions in Zimbabwe Facing Starvation After Severe Droughts, UN Food Agency Says," CNN, August 7, 2019.

[5]   Author interview, Harare, Zimbabwe, July 29, 2019.

ued thereafter and reached levels of 1:16 in August 2019. In June 2019, the government banned all use of other currencies except for the RTGS. The move to the RTGS currency and its subsequent devaluation cut salaries and purchasing power by at least tenfold, meaning that Zimbabweans' savings accounts have largely been wiped out twice in the past two decades. Wildly fluctuating exchange rates and a robust parallel market has also led to widespread currency arbitrage, with those who have access to foreign exchange (often government officials) reaping large profits.[6] Inflation has also soared. Inflation rates reached 175 percent in July 2019 before the government abruptly stopped publishing official statistics. In August 2019, the International Monetary Fund put inflation rates at 300 percent.[7] Steve Hanke, a professor at Johns Hopkins University in Baltimore, Maryland, has asserted that the real rates are much higher. In September 2019, he estimated that inflation was actually as high as 723 percent.[8]

Many interviewees emphasized Zimbabweans' acute distrust of the government regarding management of the economy and the new currency regime. After decades of monetary and fiscal mismanagement, record levels of inflation, rampant corruption, and slashed savings accounts, Zimbabweans have approached the recent switch back to a national currency with extreme trepidation. Instead of forking over their foreign exchange as the government has requested, Zimbabweans are instead holding on to scarce U.S. dollars. A Zimbabwean business leader noted that you "cannot lend money without security, security is all about confidence. In Zimbabwe today, there is no confidence."[9]

---

[6] Author interviews, Harare, Zimbabwe, July 25–August 3, 2019.

[7] International Monetary Fund, "IMF Staff Concludes Visit for the Article IV Consultation and Discussions on the First Review of the Staff-Monitored Program to Zimbabwe," press release No. 19/355, Washington, D.C., September 26, 2019.

[8] Steve Hanke, "#Zimbabwe's inflation rate has soared passed the 700%/yr barrier today. By my measure, which is the only available measure since Zimbabwe stopped producing annual inflation statistics, is 723%/yr. #Inflation is out of control in Zim, & the govt fails to adequately acknowledge it," Twitter post, September 10, 2019.

[9] Author interview, Harare, Zimbabwe, July 28, 2019.

Corruption

Corruption has historically played a key role in Zimbabwe's cartelized and patronage-based economy. In 2016, Mugabe himself claimed that Zimbabwe had lost $15 billion in mining revenue alone to corruption.[10] Mnangagwa made the fight against corruption a central pillar of his reform efforts. The Zimbabwe Anti-Corruption Commission (ZACC), stood up in the early 2000s, lacks independence and has few enforcement powers. It is headed by Loice Matanda-Moyo, who is married to Sibusiso Moyo, the foreign minister and a close ally of the president.[11] In May 2018, Mnangagwa created an anticorruption unit in the Office of the President, raising questions about independence and overlaps with the duties of the ZACC.[12]

Despite a few arrests, including of Tourism Minister Prisca Mupfumira in July 2019, corruption remains widespread under Mnangagwa. In July 2019, Zimbabwe's auditor released reports outlining massive mismanagement and corruption. Zimbabwe ranks 160 out of 180 countries on Transparency International's corruption perceptions index.[13] In October 2019, the U.S. ambassador to Zimbabwe, Brian Nichols, said that corruption was the number one cause of the economic collapse in Zimbabwe, costing the country more than $1 billion a year.[14] Mnangagwa's corruption fight appears to be highly selective, with measures focused largely on allies of Mugabe and the G40 faction of ZANU-PF. No significant steps have been taken on corruption that would directly affect the ruling or military elites closest to Mnangagwa. A senior opposition official said that Mnangagwa's fight against corruption is "a charade to sacrifice ministers not allied to him."[15] Writing

---

[10]   "Missing $15bn Diamond Revenue: Fears Mugabe Might Spill the Beans," News24, June 4, 2018.

[11]   MacDonald Dzirutwe, "Zimbabwe Vice President's Wife Arrested for Suspected Fraud, Money Laundering," Reuters, December 15, 2019.

[12]   Freedom House, 2019.

[13]   Transparency International, "Zimbabwe," webpage, undated.

[14]   Brian Nichols, "In Conversation with Trevor," video, YouTube, October 21, 2019.

[15]   Author interview, Harare, Zimbabwe, July 31, 2019.

in July 2019, Alex Magaisa, a former adviser to Tsangirai, said that the fight against corruption has been "woefully disappointing."[16]

Land

Agriculture was long the backbone of Zimbabwe's economy and land reform is a highly contentious issue in Zimbabwe. At independence, a small group of white farmers owned most of Zimbabwe's arable land, an imbalance that persisted. In the early 2000s, approximately 4,000 white farmers were evicted from their farms, often violently. The government promised to compensate farmers who had land expropriated without compensation under Mugabe's fast-track land reform program. But few funds have been dispersed and limited progress has been made on the issue of bankable leases and security of tenure, which are key to securing investment. A land audit is underway but has not been completed. The government intervened to stop a land eviction in July 2019, but land invasions continue.[17]

Although the government has taken some initial steps toward changing land policies, the issue of land reform remains far from resolved. A government minister admitted as much, saying that the issue of land remains a "work in progress." In July 2019, the minister noted that the government expects to resolve the issue of 99-year bankable leases within approximately six months.[18] The issue of nonbankable leases continues to scare off investment, because without them the government can take over land at will. An international official working on financial issues in Zimbabwe said: "The current leases are still not bankable and many do not want to invest in land that can be taken over."[19]

---

[16] Alex Magaisa, "Looters' Paradise—Zimbabwe's Road to Perdition," *Big Saturday Read*, July 20, 2019.

[17] Tonderayi Mukeredzi, "Zimbabwe's New Land Reforms Don't Go Far Enough," *Foreign Policy*, July 31, 2019.

[18] Author interview, Harare, Zimbabwe, July 30, 2019.

[19] Author interview, Harare, Zimbabwe, July 30, 2019.

Mining

Mining also plays an outsize role in Zimbabwe's economy. The country has large deposits of gold, platinum, diamonds, copper, nickel, and tin, among others. Zimbabwe's military and security officials became deeply involved in the mining sector under Mugabe, as illustrated by the Marange diamond fields, where they were implicated in widespread human rights abuses.[20] In 2008, Mugabe's government signed into law the controversial Indigenization and Empowerment Act, which required foreign-owned companies to have at least 51 percent of shares owned by indigenous black Zimbabweans.

In March 2018, Mnangagwa's administration amended the act, removing this restriction on all but platinum and diamonds, which the government said would remain because of their strategic importance. In August 2019, the government announced that they would repeal and replace the act altogether. Because of concerns from investors, in June 2019, Zimbabwe's military backed out of a $4 billion platinum joint venture with Russian investors.[21] Despite some progress on repealing the Indigenization and Empowerment Act, Zimbabwe's mining sector remains opaque, military involvement remains, and allegations of rights abuses continue. Indeed, in October 2019, the United States banned imports of Zimbabwe's rough diamonds, citing forced labor and other human rights abuses.[22]

Privatization

In early January 2018, Mnangagwa announced intentions to privatize several of the 107 state-owned enterprises, including the national airline and power utility. In May 2019, the government pledged to privatize 47 such enterprises. However, little actual progress has occurred. The government has faced issues attracting investors because many of

---

[20] Human Rights Watch, *Diamonds in the Rough: Human Rights Abuses in the Marange Diamond Fields of Zimbabwe*, New York, June 26, 2009.

[21] Kuda Chideme, "Army Offloads Stake in $4bn Project," *The Standard*, June 23, 2019.

[22] "Does Zimbabwe Have Forced Labour in its Diamond Mines?" BBC News, October 20, 2019.

the entities are defunct or bankrupt. In 2016, 38 parastatal companies[23] had losses of $270 million. In July 2018, state-owned enterprises and parastatal companies owed taxes of $491 million.[24] Few of the privatization deadlines outlined under Minister of Finance Mthuli Ncube's Transitional Stabilisation Programme have been met, including those for Agribank, the Grain Marketing Board, and the Zimbabwe Power Company. According to Zimbabwean economist and former official Eddie Cross, lack of progress on privatization is "a great disappointment and the consequences to the fiscus are huge. . . . Many investors see us as an unstable destination. We can overcome this if we offer better investment conditions."[25]

Political Interference and Rivalry

For decades, Zimbabwe's patronage-based economy meant that economic fortunes were determined not by business acumen or market forces but by political allegiance to the ruling party. Mnangagwa has made little to no progress in moving Zimbabwe away from this practice, in which political elites pick winners and losers to suit their political and personal interests. Indeed, interviews revealed that political interference continues to hamper Zimbabwe's economy and may be increasing in certain quarters, particularly in agriculture and fuel. According to an international official working on financial issues, economic decisions are often made outside official channels, with vested interests interfering in government policy. The official said political "interference is everywhere" in the economy.[26] An opposition official echoed this sentiment, saying that the government "wants to pick winners, so some sectors are not allowed to fail, they are too big to fail, if

---

[23] According to the Cambridge Dictionary, *parastatal* is "used to describe a company or organization which is owned by a country's government and often has some political power" (Cambridge Dictionary, "Parastatal," webpage, undated).

[24] Tatira Zwinoira, "Parastatals to be Privatised in Six Months, Says Official," *The Standard*, May 12, 2019.

[25] Fidelity Mhlanga, "Government Misses Privatisation Deadlines," *The Standard*, October 6, 2019.

[26] Author interview, Harare, Zimbabwe, July 30, 2019.

big politically."[27] Continued political interference in the economy suggests that, in many important areas, economic incentives are aligned against any genuine reform, a dynamic that is unlikely to shift under current leadership.

There also appears to be emerging intraministerial and intraparty rifts over economic policy, whereby the economic reform efforts of the Ministry of Finance are often constrained by the Reserve Bank.[28] The Ministry of Finance, led by Ncube, largely appears to be trying to implement sound economic policies, starting with tightening government spending and taking initial steps to move toward a more liberalized economy. However, Ncube's efforts are being thwarted by the Reserve Bank and other hardliners in the government. This faction is headed by central bank Governor John Mangudya, who represents the old way of doing business under the highly subsidized economy. Interviews revealed that Mnangagwa often sides with the more assertive Mangudya during Cabinet meetings.[29] According to a Mnangagwa adviser, Ncube thinks he is "not moving fast enough, but Mnangagwa thinks he is moving too fast."[30]

Conclusion

In short, despite some progress in certain areas, Mnangagwa's economic reform efforts are incomplete or falling short across a variety of sectors, including the new currency regime, inflation, corruption, land, mining, and privatization. Rampant political interference and intraparty splits are also hampering progress. Indeed, given Zimbabwe's enduring patronage-based economy, where economic fortunes continue to be determined not by business acumen but by allegiance to ZANU-PF politicians, politics and economics cannot be separated in Zimbabwe. As an adviser to Mnangagwa put it: "Politics dictates and

---

[27] Author interview, Harare, Zimbabwe, July 30, 2019.

[28] Author interviews, Harare, Zimbabwe, July 25–August 3, 2019.

[29] Author interviews, Harare, Zimbabwe, July 25–August 3, 2019.

[30] Author interview, Harare, Zimbabwe, July 26, 2019.

distorts economics" in Zimbabwe.[31] As argued by a Zimbabwean business leader, economic reform efforts will not "be successful without addressing the underlying political problems plaguing the country."[32] An opposition figure placed the failure to change the direction of the economy directly at the feet of Mnangagwa, saying that the leader is primarily driven by his own economic self-interest. One interviewee quipped that Mnangagwa "is not the president of Zimbabwe but of his own bottom line."[33]

---

[31]   Author interview, Harare, Zimbabwe, July 26, 2019.

[32]   Author interview, Harare, Zimbabwe, July 29, 2019.

[33]   Author interview, Harare, Zimbabwe, July 29, 2019.

CHAPTER FOUR

Conclusion: Forecast and Recommendations

Forecast

Politics and economics are inextricably linked in Zimbabwe. With the old guard and the military still firmly in power—and benefiting from their perch atop the highly cartelized and patronage-based economy—under present conditions, genuine reform is unlikely in the next one to three years. Zimbabwe is likely to continue down a path of political polarization, protests, political violence at the hands of the state, and economic deterioration.

A much-discussed national dialogue to resolve the current political crisis is unlikely to bear fruit in the short term because of entrenched positions on both sides of the political spectrum. Mnangagwa will need to continue to carefully navigate factional disputes between his old guard and newer technocrats in the party, particularly on the economic front. However, as long as Mnangagwa does not cross his military backers or become deeply unpopular in the run-up to elections, he is likely to remain in power and will be the favorite in the 2023 vote. The military is unlikely to relinquish its ascendant power without a fight and, therefore, will likely endure as a political kingmaker for years to come. Unless Mnangagwa becomes exceedingly unpopular or takes aim at the military, the risk of a coup is real but moderate under current circumstances.

Zimbabwe's opposition, led by Nelson Chamisa of the MDC, is constrained by frequent arrests, harassment, and abductions by security forces, along with a lack of resources and grassroots organizing structures. The MDC is likely to continue to stage demonstrations in urban strongholds but, under current conditions, will likely remain unable to mobilize countrywide protests that could put significant pressure on the government. This dynamic could change if the opposition is able to build a more cohesive, nationwide organization that could tap into growing discontent with the economic situation. Protests are likely to continue to be suppressed violently by security forces.

Without fundamental reforms that would end political interference and unlock international support, economic conditions are likely to continue to deteriorate, exacerbated—especially in the short term—by ongoing drought and a sharp decrease in consumer demand. If current conditions hold, Zimbabwe is likely to see continued inflation, currency depreciation, price increases, and limited growth over the next one to three years.[1] GDP growth, currently at −7 percent, is likely to rebound to the 2–3 percent range once the drought is over. Yet price increases and shortages of power, fuel, and food are likely to continue to spark demonstrations, particularly in urban areas. Given the expected lack of genuine reforms, international sanctions are likely to remain in place.

Investment in Zimbabwe is high risk, which will continue to deter potential investors in the near term. If investors have a high risk tolerance, there are certainly opportunities, particularly in services and agriculture. Although government officials enthusiastically called for an influx of investment, a common refrain from business leaders, the opposition, and civil society actors interviewed for this study was "wait" or "stay away, for now." Other interviewees were more critical, saying, "You'd be crazy."[2] A few interviewees suggested that potential investors should carefully consider the public relations effects of being seen to support the current government, especially during ongoing waves of repression and political violence.[3]

---

[1] World Bank, undated; International Monetary Fund, "Zimbabwe," webpage, undated; Economist Intelligence Unit, "Zimbabwe," webpage, undated.

[2] Author interviews, Harare, Zimbabwe, July 25–August 3, 2019.

[3] Author interviews, Harare, Zimbabwe, July 25–August 3, 2019.

Recommendations

Zimbabwe has tremendous potential, with rich natural resources and one of the most educated populations in Africa. To help support the country's recovery from decades of mismanagement, corruption, and state violence, international actors—including the United States—would be wise to push the government in a coordinated fashion to implement genuine political, economic, and security reforms. Such reforms would go a long way toward putting Zimbabwe on a democratic path, lowering levels of political polarization, and repairing the collapsing economy. Reforms would also reassure potential investors and help to earn back the goodwill—and possible access to lending—of the international community.

Although Zimbabwe does not have much strategic value to the United States, America is the largest bilateral donor to Zimbabwe and holds some leverage. According to U.S. Ambassador to Zimbabwe Nichols, the United States has given $3.2 billion to Zimbabwe since independence, including $300 million in 2019.[4] The United States should continue to urge the Zimbabwean government to honor its reform pledges. A good starting point would be pushing the government to respect its own constitution, allow for peaceful protest, fully repeal repressive laws, and hold security forces accountable for human rights abuses and the killing of unarmed civilians. International democracy and governance assistance should be increased, with a particular focus on professionalizing political parties. A cooling-off period of one to five years before military officials can join politics would also help to disincentivize more coups and security sector involvement in political processes.

---

[4]   Nichols, 2019.

The international community should proceed with extreme caution on economic support for the government. International actors should

- set clear benchmarks that would indicate progress on economic reform (the Millennium Challenge Cooperation indicators[5] might provide a useful template)
- withhold support for debt relief or any new lending until clear and unambiguous progress has been made on political and economic reforms and respect for human rights
- begin planning for possible private-sector activities, such as reopening business at the Overseas Private Investment Corporation or the U.S. Trade and Development Agency
- closely track the fight against corruption, looking for signs that prosecutions are more than politically motivated
- provide legal and financial support for efforts to identify and recover stolen assets.

Conclusion

In sum, although Mnangagwa has repeatedly deployed flowery reform rhetoric, his administration's piecemeal actions belie any movement toward genuine political or economic reform. Repression has increased, and the economy continues to sink. The Mnangagwa government has taken some modest steps that could be seen as an indication of progress—particularly on the economic front. But politics and economics are inseparable in Zimbabwe, and the country will be unable to recover unless the two sectors are addressed in tandem. There is a wide gap between the government's reform rhetoric and the reality on the ground. The government's well-rehearsed slogans appear to be largely political theater targeted at the international diplomatic community and potential investors. Even where limited progress has been made,

---

5   Millennium Challenge Cooperation, "Selection Indicators," webpage, undated.

such steps appear to be largely cosmetic, a mere box-ticking exercise. In other words, Mnangagwa is attempting to have his cake and eat it too, paying lip service to reforms in the hope of securing international support but staunchly refusing to implement any measures that might harm his and his closest supporters' political and economic interests.

References

Afrobarometer and Mass Public Opinion Institute, "Zimbabweans Remain Apprehensive About Manipulation of the Presidential Election, New Survey Finds," press release, Harare, Zimbabwe, July 23, 2018. As of November 1, 2019:
https://afrobarometer.org/sites/default/files/press-release/Zimbabwe/zim_r7.5_pr2_zimbabweans_remain_apprehensive_about_election_manipulation_23072018.pdf

Beamer, Glenn, "Elite Interviews and State Politics Research," *State Politics and Policy Quarterly*, Vol. 2, No. 1, Spring 2002.

Beardsworth, Nicole, Nic Cheeseman, and Simukai Tinhu, "Zimbabwe: The Coup That Never Was, and the Election That Could Have Been," *African Affairs*, Vol. 118, No. 472, September 2019, pp. 580–596.

Biti, Tendai, "History Repeats Itself in Zimbabwe," *Foreign Affairs*, August 20, 2019. As of November 1, 2019:
https://www.foreignaffairs.com/articles/africa/2019-08-20/history-repeats-itself-zimbabwe

Cambridge Dictionary, "Parastatal," webpage, undated. As of January 24, 2020:
https://dictionary.cambridge.org/us/dictionary/english/parastatal

Catholic Commission for Justice and Peace, *Breaking the Silence, Building True Peace: A Report on the Disturbances in Matabeleland and the Midlands, 1980 to 1988 Summary Report*, Harare, Zimbabwe: Legal Resources Foundation, 1999.

Chideme, Kuda, "Army Offloads Stake in $4bn Project," *The Standard*, June 23, 2019. As of November 1, 2019:
https://www.thestandard.co.zw/2019/06/23/army-offloads-stake-4bn-project/

Chingono, Mark, and Bukola Adebayo, "Millions in Zimbabwe Facing Starvation After Severe Droughts, UN Food Agency Says," CNN, August 7, 2019. As of November 1, 2019:
https://www.cnn.com/2019/08/07/africa/zimbabwe-millions-starvation-intl/index.html

"Does Zimbabwe Have Forced Labour in its Diamond Mines?" BBC News, October 20, 2019. As of November 1, 2019:
https://www.bbc.com/news/world-africa-49998494

Dzirutwe, MacDonald, "Zimbabwe Rebases Data, Boosting GDP Numbers by 40 Pct," Reuters, October 5, 2018. As of October 31, 2019:
https://www.reuters.com/article/zimbabwe-economy/
update-2-zimbabwe-rebases-data-boosting-gdp-numbers-by-40-pct-idUSL8N1WL1YM

———, "Zimbabwe Vice President's Wife Arrested for Suspected Fraud, Money Laundering," Reuters, December 15, 2019. As of December 19, 2019:
https://www.usnews.com/news/world/articles/2019-12-15/
zimbabwe-vice-presidents-wife-arrested-for-suspected-fraud-money-laundering

Economist Intelligence Unit, "Zimbabwe," webpage, undated. As of December 19, 2019:
https://country.eiu.com/zimbabwe

Freedom House, "Zimbabwe," Washington, D.C., *Freedom in the World 2019*, February 2019. As of November 1, 2019:
https://freedomhouse.org/report/freedom-world/2019/zimbabwe

Hanke, Steve, "#Zimbabwe's inflation rate has soared passed the 700%/yr barrier today. By my measure, which is the only available measure since Zimbabwe stopped producing annual inflation statistics, is 723%/yr. #Inflation is out of control in Zim, & the govt fails to adequately acknowledge it," Twitter post, September 10, 2019. As of January 23, 2020:
https://twitter.com/steve_hanke/status/1171463820545409024?lang=en

Human Rights Watch, *Diamonds in the Rough: Human Rights Abuses in the Marange Diamond Fields of Zimbabwe*, New York, June 26, 2009. As of November 1, 2019:
http://www.hrw.org/en/reports/2009/06/26/diamonds-rough

———, *Perpetual Fear: Impunity and Cycles of Violence in Zimbabwe*, New York, March 8, 2011. As of October 31, 2019:
https://www.hrw.org/report/2011/03/08/perpetual-fear/
impunity-and-cycles-violence-zimbabwe

———, "Zimbabwe: Excessive Force Used Against Protesters," webpage, March 12, 2019. As of November 1, 2019:
https://www.hrw.org/news/2019/03/12/
zimbabwe-excessive-force-used-against-protesters#

International Monetary Fund, "IMF Staff Concludes Visit for the Article IV Consultation and Discussions on the First Review of the Staff-Monitored Program to Zimbabwe," press release No. 19/355, Washington, D.C., September 26, 2019. As of October 31, 2019:
https://www.imf.org/en/News/Articles/2019/09/26/pr19355-zimbabwe-imf-staff-concludes-visit-art-consult-discuss-1st-rev-staff-mon-program

————, "Zimbabwe," webpage, undated. As of December 19, 2019:
https://www.imf.org/en/Countries/ZWE

International Republican Institute and National Democratic Institute, *IRI/NDI Zimbabwe International Election Observation Mission: Final Report*, Washington, D.C., October 2018. As of November 1, 2019:
https://www.ndi.org/sites/default/files/2018-10-29%20Final%20ZIEOM%20 Report%20%288MB%29.pdf

Jackson, Paul, "The Civil War Roots of Military Domination in Zimbabwe: The Integration Process Following the Rhodesian War and the Road to ZANLA Dominance," *Civil Wars*, Vol. 13, No. 4, 2011, pp. 371–395.

Magaisa, Alex, "Looters' Paradise—Zimbabwe's Road to Perdition," *Big Saturday Read*, July 20, 2019. As of November 1, 2019:
https://www.bigsr.co.uk/single-post/2019/07/20/ Big-Saturday-Read-Looters-Paradise--Road-to-Perdition

Mavedzenge, Justice Alfred, "Is Zimbabwe's President Mnangagwa Using Constitutional Amendments to Rig the 2023 Elections?" *Democracy in Africa*, January 22, 2020. As of January 29, 2020:
http://democracyinafrica.org/zimbabwes-president-mnangagwa-using-constitutional-amendments-rig-2023-elections/

Mhlanga, Fidelity, "Government Misses Privatisation Deadlines," *The Standard*, October 6, 2019. As of November 1, 2019:
https://www.thestandard.co.zw/2019/10/06/ government-misses-privatisation-deadlines/

Millennium Challenge Cooperation, "Selection Indicators," webpage, undated. As of January 24, 2020:
https://www.mcc.gov/who-we-fund/indicators

"Missing $15bn Diamond Revenue: Fears Mugabe Might Spill the Beans," News24, June 4, 2018. As of November 1, 2019:
https://www.news24.com/Africa/Zimbabwe/ missing-15bn-diamond-revenue-fears-mugabe-might-spill-the-beans-20180604

Mukeredzi, Tonderayi, "Zimbabwe's New Land Reforms Don't Go Far Enough," *Foreign Policy*, July 31, 2019. As of November 1, 2019:
https://foreignpolicy.com/2019/07/31/zimbabwes-new-land-reforms-dont-go-far-enough-mugabe-mnangagwa-white-farmers/

Nichols, Brian, "In Conversation with Trevor," video, YouTube, October 21, 2019. As of November 1, 2019:
https://www.youtube.com/watch?v=_RudQyah7WI

Noyes, Alexander, "*Plus ça Change*? The Dynamics of Security Sector Reform in Zimbabwe, 2009–2013," in Blessing-Miles Tendi, Jocelyn Alexander, and JoAnn McGregor, eds., *The Oxford Handbook of Zimbabwean Studies*, Oxford, UK: Oxford University Press, forthcoming.

Quest, Richard, and Sheena McKenzie, "President Mnangagwa: Zimbabwe Is Open for Business," CNN, January 24, 2018. As of November 1, 2019: https://www.cnn.com/2018/01/24/africa/zimbabwe-president-emmerson-mnangagwa-davos-intl/index.html

Rutherford, Blair, "Mugabe's Shadow: Limning the Penumbrae of Post-Coup Zimbabwe," *Canadian Journal of African Studies*, Vol. 52, No. 1, 2018, pp. 53–68.

Tendi, Blessing-Miles, "Robert Mugabe and Toxicity: History and Context Matter," *Representation*, Vol. 47, No. 3, 2011, pp. 307–318.

———, "The Motivations and Dynamics of Zimbabwe's 2017 Military Coup," *African Affairs*, October 28, 2019, pp. 1–29.

Transparency International, "Zimbabwe," webpage, undated. As of November 1, 2019: https://www.transparency.org/country/ZWE

World Bank, "Zimbabwe," webpage, undated. As of October 31, 2019: https://data.worldbank.org/country/zimbabwe

"Zimbabwe Is Open for Business: Mnangagwa," SABC News, December 21, 2017. As of January 10, 2020: http://www.sabcnews.com/sabcnews/zimbabwe-open-business-mnagangwa/

Zwinoira, Tatira, "Parastatals to be Privatised in Six Months, Says Official," *The Standard*, May 12, 2019. As of November 1, 2019: https://www.thestandard.co.zw/2019/05/12/parastatals-privatised-six-months-says-official/

Caitlin Press Inc.
8100 Alderwood Road,
Halfmoon Bay, BC V0N 1Y1
www.caitlin-press.com

Text design by Jakelene Plan
Cover design by Vici Johnstone
Cover image by Suzo Hickey, www.suzohickey.ca
Printed in Canada

Caitlin Press Inc. acknowledges financial support from the Government of Canada and the Canada Council for the Arts, and the Province of British Columbia through the British Columbia Arts Council and the Book Publisher's Tax Credit.

Library and Archives Canada Cataloguing in Publication

Byers, Jane, 1966-, author
    Acquired community / Jane Byers.

Poems.
ISBN 978-1-987915-22-8 (paperback)

    I. Title.

PS8603.Y47A64 2016   C811'.6   C2016-903636-7